Jargon 83

poems by Thomas Meyer

with drawings by Paul Sinodhinos

THE UMBRELLA OF AESCULAPIUS

the Jargon Society
Highlands, North Carolina   *1975*

I wrote the poems between summer 1966 & late autumn 1970. Their order herein approximately that. Some appeared in these magazines whose editors I thank: *Caterpillar*, Clayton Eshleman; *The Lampeter Muse*, Peter Boffey; *Sumac*, Dan Gerber; *Tansy*, John Moritz. The *Finial* & *Stonewall* presses at Urbana issued 'Poikilos' as a small book, 250 copies.

Designed by Alvin Doyle Moore

Printed by Superior Printing Company, Champaign, Illinois 61820

Manufactured in the United States of America

Distributed by
The Book Organization,
Elm Street
Millerton, New York 12546

Jonathan's

ὥs τε, μέλημα τὦμον,

περπτύγω

AN INTRODUCTION TO THIS BOOK OF THOMAS MEYER'S.

yo usrānām apīcyā
veda nāmāni guhyā
sa kaviḥ kāvyā puru
rūpaṃ dyaur iva puṣyati

> *he who knows the secret*
> *hidden names of the cows*
> *as a poet/seer he greatly prospers poetic art*
> *as the bright sky its color*

(Ṛg-Veda 8.41.5, cited and translated by Calvert Watkins in his essay "Language of gods, language of men," in *Myth and Law among the Indo-Europeans*, ed. Puhvel, Berkeley, 1970.)

■

Who will preserve the old names, not as lore in aging books (for all my love of books) but will set them to dance in the new days,

the new discourse we have after all (Amerikanoi!) fashioned?
Is there a contradiction here, one we want to weep or wrangle, say, between the beautiful precisions that have been preserved for us in old records, old poems,

and this new, necessary, sense now advancing from the powerful productivities of Pound, Olson, Zukofsky and those who have learned from them?

This sense demands the clarity possible only when a man speaks from his own experienced body, his own breath (as our song goes), size of the world about him what he can in fact touch with his feet, his swung arms:

the perhaps natural sentimental restoration (o dated now, a public thing now, but not long ago a sharp excitement, reaffirming us) of the Body as center,

how does that sense do combat with the old words, the natural unhumanized (it would seem) events (the flower, the stream, the beast under the hedge) in fact deeply humanized, dream-realized, by the names we have laid upon them

or recovered from their shapes or behaviors in a trance of our own attentions

or caught from the old books, names, words, old ways of talking the world into place?

Combat or concert?

What excites me here is a continually sustained dialectic between an holistic sense of language (=English in all her times, Maldon to Altamont)

and a refreshed (but equally holistic) sense of the poem as existential process.

Most of our great innovators (but not Pound, or Bunting across the water) were suspicious of the old words, the 'poetic' words, in turn of the 'poetic' things themselves, as if every creature but man were a captive in an arid poetic zoo—

and rightly enough were suspicious, in favor of their concentration on the Now of the poem's coming into being. But the poem does not come into being far away from the mind, and the mind, good mind, is alive with all the instances of naming and singing, old and new, that have borne in upon it.

In Meyer's work, then, I find a type of the above: dialectic of the historic and the existential (to use words tireder than his own) right in the fact of the single poem, a dialectic that is not resolved by, but does, in deed, resolve the poem.

And that's our contemporary marvel, that we have set forth (in the words of a recent correspondent) a new discourse:

> "whose problems—language problems—have been largely
> solved, to the extent that even my students quickly master
> them. . . . We *do* have a language which is more responsive
> than any we've had since the 17th century."
> (Don Byrd, letter of December 1973)

The austere exercises of craft and skill seem to have prepared us to unite our *times* again. To move in all the times of our mind.

And this language, solvable but not easy, is one I find Meyer working through. Responsive? The new language so, yes, because a language is not its lexicon, and the lexicon of our attentions can feed, now, the enriched complexity of mental act the poem now can be:

I open *The Umbrella of Aesculapius* (the name is a stretto of all these themes here striven), and I find:

> *Gorgon-headed candied sea holly*
> *has an adder's hue,*
> *eyes & nose*
> *that make a man a mirror*
> *& when you gather it*
> *(root & wort)*
> *let no sun*
> *shine on it*
> *Light steals the color of its power).*

And I ponder this instruction, or as instruction. If the old words (Gorgon, holly, adder, wort) are good for anything

(not as helps in reading old poems only), then they are words still, word here being utterance,

an outer articulation of what is (suddenly!) experienced.

Good for anything.

They store the power of long attention to things in the world,

and on them we draw. They bring us too the fruits of a kingdom that seems to vanish from our sight day by day,

and the lost possibilities (ecology!) of knowing in the senses are recruited, won, for the world of the mind, the knower, knower of this field,

As ever, then, accumulation and discharge.

But the way the lines fall, above, demands our notice, the dwindling measure of the first eight lines all at once rapt and quickened with "Light steals the color of its power," outrageous that words of such vagrancy (light, color, power), weak words, can here be wielded *as* powers, can be powerful, caught in the quickening dance itself the apparently meek preceding accuracies prepared.

∎

Dance? The image of dance has haunted poetics at least since Yeats and Charles Williams and William Carlos Williams. Each age of poetry seems to have a pet metaphor drawn from other arts for an inward vision of its own nature; so in the sixteenth the stage, seventeenth the choir, eighteenth the senate or the coffee-house, so in our century we seem to have toyed with the image of ourselves as dancers and our shared work as a most complex dance. Clearest here to me is Duncan's offering of the 'attend/dance'—the poet's constant attention to the behavior of phonemes and syllables in the very act of his articulation, 'vowel-leading,' following the tones in (what we would love to describe as) the words' own way. Writing the poem, then, is discovery, *trobar*, finding the music and cooperating with the linguistic event—a dance sometimes of standing aside.

Dance? Perhaps the metaphor is obsolescent, or gradually turns into an image of the poet as scientist, with mind, heartmind, eye all fixed on the work "under hand." Dance or not dance, I point to something that would describe what the sounds of words *do*. How they lead and defer to one another, or how a word hurries in and blocks with its sharp vowel a whole chain of darker metaphones. Metaphony. Beyond the gap of "word" or even syntax. Dance, why not, the light limbs of the lovers as a metaphor for the air we breathe into our own intricate passages, air that takes shape and color there, returns to the world to say what process it has moved through and now restores to the public air.

Following Meyer's traces, I'm dazzled by the daring of a quatrain like this one, on Egyptian Neith:

> *I've been, am, will be*
> *yet no man's drawn my net apart.*
> *My shuttle wove the world,*
> *I bore the sun before the born.*

where on the last sound itself (a word, too, provocatively used, forcing full consciousness of all it means, and does not mean), all the preceding dozen syllables converge, resound, as if they'd found the single Tonic of their system.

■

When I read such work (and perhaps that's Pound's *sinceritas* working again), I want to believe whatever a man tells me who tells it that alertly. I will credit his predicament and his passion, come at length perhaps even to trust him that the gods and flowers and lovers are not just names in a book, needing glosses or sweat. They are names in *his* book, a glad book, fine instance of the life of process brought to, life.

Robert Kelly

Annandale, February 1974

della Francesca

Your eyes,
Piero,
according to their term,
grow smaller or greater.
Rocks surround me,
Piero,
lead me from this place.

I   black   .   bituminous
                          twice born

□□□□□□□□□□□□□□□□□□□□□□□□□□□□□□□□□

one thousand years old,
       turned to coal
by the secret's pressure

□□□□□□□□□□□□□□□□□□□□□□□□□□□□□□□□□□

fruit, peaches & pears

Winged feet,
       purple banks
       above water
             twice born
       of sea-water.

□□□□□□□□□□□□□□□□□□□□□□□□□□□□□□□□□□

to whom
is cedar sacred?

of whom
is Neptune patron?

□□□□□□□□□□□□□□□□□□□□□□□□□□□□□□□□□□

an economy:
the trade of goods,
gifts from the gods.

□□□□□□□□□□□□□□□□□□□□□□□□□□□□□□□□□□

        faggots,

the flames' light forming a fabric,
all things. Fire of their flesh

bronze, blond, gold, twice born,
twice the fire, the flame, the coal,

heats' keepe

□□□□□□□□□□□□□□□□□□□□□□□□□□□□□□□□□□

        1 bronze basin
        2 bronze flagons
        2 bronze fonts

1 ladle, 1 cup, 1 knife

1 linen wrap, washed,
1 clay-colored cloak for winter.

Bags of meal,
cereals & bran, barley,
jugs with honey in them.

Coal, two lumps,
one hard, one soft
for the fire.

. . . purple flowers for their shoulders
      (the gift of a hip
        from the hedgerow)

Pumice (porous), stone for the foot,
papyrus, papyri, paper & a flask.

      (the line of his hip)
puma, the sleek, hermetic beast
      (the gift of his hip)

   O puma,
        sacred to Hermes . . .

white lady or lion.

Cattle driver,
      dream bringer,
           watcher by night.

□□□□□□□□□□□□□□□□□□□□□□□□□□□□□□□□□□

Light in the honey,
        the liquid falls like Demeter's hair.
Maya, mother & temple
               of all.

      She moves
            the veil
                  her subtle light

□□□□□□□□□□□□□□□□□□□□□□□□□□□□□□□□□□□□

Enough oil for the lamps of light
       & fish for his service. Christ,

master of sun, his white flesh
       made blue by the clay of his sepulchre.

□□□□□□□□□□□□□□□□□□□□□□□□□□□□□□□□□□□

     The logos of the beast
beyond the mind of the elders.

        In the vessels the wine is made ready,

their grain winnowed & ground.

□□□□□□□□□□□□□□□□□□□□□□□□□□□□□□□□□□□□

This is the fish of his flesh
        the wine of his flagon
& bread from his mouth

to eat, to drink, to take.

□□□□□□□□□□□□□□□□□□□□□□□□□□□□□□□□□□□□□

   & the people
       went to sea,
dug the hill & grew
olive, grape.

□□□□□□□□□□□□□□□□□□□□□□□□□□□□□□□□□□□□□□□

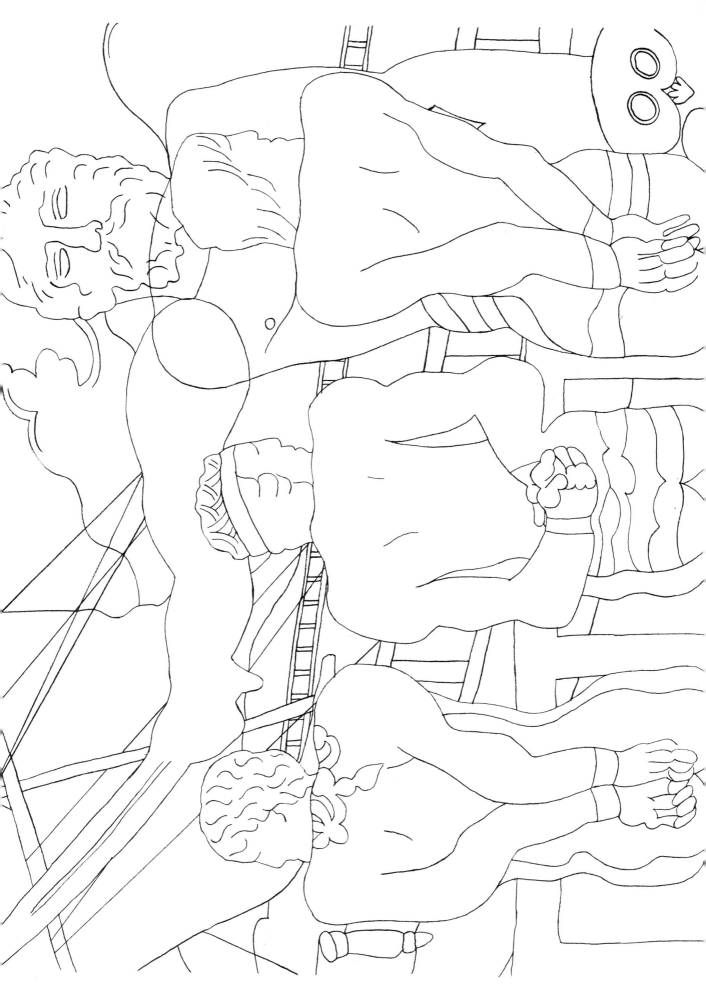

          Sophia, Satan, Iacchus,
Christos, befriend light.

□□□□□□□□□□□□□□□□□□□□□□□□□□□□□□□□□□

Fire-sticks
          or tally-sticks

□□□□□□□□□□□□□□□□□□□□□□□□□□□□□□□□□□

twice born of wine
& black waters

□□□□□□□□□□□□□□□□□□□□□□□□□□□□□□□□□□

a great ball
          & thread of light

□□□□□□□□□□□□□□□□□□□□□□□□□□□□□□□□□□

Themistocles, the commander-in-chief, wishing to ensure victory for his
side, offered three human victims as sacrifice to Dionysus, *eater of raw
flesh*. These were three young prisoners of great beauty, magnificently
attired, adorned with golden jewels, the nephews of the Great King
himself. The general slew them with his own hand, on the flagship, in
the presence of the whole fleet. It was not an act of reprisal but a solemn
consecration.

                    blood on the water

□□□□□□□□□□□□□□□□□□□□□□□□□□□□□□□□□□

Turn of their loins
& curve of the chest,

               nipples, down
               on the arm & slight

hair on the leg,

the line of the calf
bends to the knee & into

    the hollow,

the grace of the spine
nestled above nates

Raw flesh for Dionysus.

□□□□□□□□□□□□□□□□□□□□□□□□□□□□□□□□□

    Fear rules their fingers,

    jewelry rings in sunlight,
        catching flames.

□□□□□□□□□□□□□□□□□□□□□□□□□□□□□□□□□

    Willow or pine, olives
        grow on the hill.

Boys
    in the heat of the sun
       shake dust
       from the grape.

Girls
    gather damp from
       the leaves of trees
       in the yard.

□□□□□□□□□□□□□□□□□□□□□□□□□□□□□□□□□

Born of the river,

the sea runs inward,
the land joins the water

    & wine fills the cup.

□□□□□□□□□□□□□□□□□□□□□□□□□□□□□□□□□

To dance at a wedding,

daktyls: four-footed beasts

      in the pastures, goats,
      sheep, the lamb & oxen

yoked,
      the cow giving milk
& her bull.

      The music,   come
      leaping fish, come

      turning vine, come food & fruit
            come drink & corn,

the wine,

come dancing feet.

□□□

II   Poseidon's arm reaches
                           inward
                           down the Hudson,
        the river is still salt
                           at Kingston.

        At his fingers float
                    John Cruger's island,
        and in his palm
                    Salamis.

        Semele dances on Hudson's waters.
        Her son sports
                    a Corinthian crown of wild celery.

             (Pindar tells us
              Corinth was a polis
              known for splendid youth.)

        Mother & Son sailed from
                    Crete, home of
                           ancient hours,

                 to the Empire
                 state, New York.

        Dead Semele, a shade beside the boy

                 receives her son
                 in Annandale,
                           off the Hudson
        & up Riverroad
                 from Barrytown.

        □□

        Navin's oral history of the area:

             "& the kid
                    floated past the Vidal
                    place
                 & the docks
                           to Cruger's

                 where he came up
                 from the waters

                           naked."

Abraham & Issac
Olson said
was a much better

myth, or example of
the pharmakon

(than those three
Persian boys. What was the state
of Bacchic worship during those odd
twenty years?)

Drive out the plague,
the result of the
female-beast: our lady
of the riddle. She
guards the gates & eats
the city's men.

A ram,
          caught

in
thicket.

Hermes, the boundary
stone. The map &

grain routes,
lines of commerce.

Coal to burn in the temple

fruit dried, meat salted

      & water, in jugs,
      for the crew,

cedar ships, cedar logs
(sacred fires) grains

et cetera, linen & flax
the temple tools
the sacred knife

oil packed tunny

      jugs of wine as well
      great

loaves & dried fruit
gold & stones

      olives

goods to bring to
city gates.

& they
set sail
in their ships.

THE GRINDSTONE

The GRINDSTONE is desire. Its turning is a way that wants an intelligent man to make a place before the door of his heart for that way to enter him. Once the GRINDSTONE has entered the heart it cannot be cast out. It overcomes the man & he becomes not only the color of the rainbow but the rainbow itself.

There is a Prince who is dreaming the way of the GRINDSTONE under the letter त. This dream began in the *Mahabharata* itself & goes on at this very moment. Vishnu is the Prince who dreams & gives the way of the GRINDSTONE to men.

The man who embraces the way of the GRINDSTONE is embraced by it. He is held by its two stones, the Washing & the Road, as a cloud is held over an ocean.

In the Prince's dream, the man who passes through the Washing passes through four reflections cast upon clear water: the Dark of the Moon; the Prohibition; the Strike Against; & the Ray of Light. The reflecting surface changes from water to fire to air, returning to the Dark of the Moon as the man watches.

When the man leaves the Washing he comes to the Road. There there are no more reflections. On the Road are four places: the Treasure House; the Dung Fallen from a Man's Mouth; the Water Jar; & the Birth.

The Washing & the Road lead to eight Cities. These Cities are not on the surface of the earth but are beneath the reflections of the Washing & the places of the Road. These Cities are like the Entrails of a beast. The City below the Dark of the Moon is Attack, so called because this is the best time for new conquests to be made. The City below Prohibition is Fiery Splendor which is the desire that increases & does not die. The City below Strike Against is Combination of the Result of the Blow, as when fire leaps from flint & steel. The City below the Ray of Light is the New Moon or the conquest begun.

The Cities of the Washing are Cities of Search & Meditation. But the Cities of the Road are Cities of Happiness & Pleasure. The City below the Treasure House is Devotion. The City under Dung is Snow. The Cities that lie beneath the Water Jug & the Birth are Deep Sleep & the God of Rain.

Like Entrails, the Cities surround a Heart. But the path between the Cities & the Heart is difficult & filled with Tears & Weeping. This path is like the Paint Brush of the poet & artist; it is difficult to tell if what comes from its strokes is true or false.

The region around the GRINDSTONE's Heart is a Wheel, the hub of which is the heart of a Ruddy Goose from which extend her wings, head & tail. These members are like the spokes of the Wheel which turns as the Goose flies from the Unobstructed to the Melting to the Eternal & to Completion.

The hub of the Wheel is the Heart of the GRINDSTONE. There lie Joy & Pleasure, the point of the Erect Lingam. For if a man were to copulate with a goose he would find his lingam at the goose's Heart.

THE UMBRELLA OF AESCULAPIUS

topoi & commentaries
in memory of Giulio Camillo

Augustine confesses:

In the plains, caves, caverns
of my memory are
innumberable things,

images, arts,
bodies, presences,
the mind's affection.

What thought can't feel
the memory keeps

& keeps in mind as well.

I run, I fly
over them all
this side & that
as far as I can

& there is no end.

I wanted to write a poem whose pace was stately & deliberate, whose reader moved as a witness, & whose lines, in clusters, revealed groups of figures in well lit niches. Such a movement coupled with such a spectacle I reasoned would impress the memory, which is to say the soul, of the reader. The classical sons of this & related arts teach us that that end may be reached by the use of the unforgettable: an extreme, or more subtly, a small but striking detail; blood stained shirt, wall-eye, or crooked finger. A hand above the fifth of the series & a cross above the tenth, these indicate order. I have abandoned them being unsure that I could truly indicate the fifth or tenth of any series. Who knows what has dropped out, drops out & is lost every time we blink an eye. I am left with the following in what seems a plausible order. They are shadow boxes, *loci*, or *topoi*, the stations of memory. What I wanted from them was nothing more or less than Giordano Bruno asked of his magic figures, or the Imagists in 1910 demanded of a poem. Honey-tongued Simonides, the first professional poet, invented memory as a livelihood, the means of all men's salvation depends upon it as well. It is wicked to speak of poems like this, but then the memories in them are not mine alone. I have provided commentaries.

Love demands I let no man move here alone.

Evans found them chatting,
fresh from their elaborate toilet,
hair frisé, wound around their heads,
tumbling down their backs
twisted with beads & jewels . . .

"But these are Parisians," these
ladies of Knossos
                              restored by Gilliéron.

That was in 1901. Their skirts were striped & colorful.

Protect the Keftiu, Isis,

      death defying goddess
                           $(\dot{\alpha}\theta\acute{\alpha}\nu\alpha\tau')$

    & quicken their hearts with aphrodisiacs.

Her popularity spread widely until she swallowed all the other gods & goddesses of Aegypt, surrounding territories, & periplus. The liberty here, glossed as such, is that she is actually less, or without death, rather than the defier of it, which one would suspect as well. Aphrodisiacs is a triple pun. Aphrodite was swallowed as well. & Aphrodisiacs are swallowed by her followers who go by the same name.

Gorgon-headed candied sea holly
has an adder's hue,
eyes & nose

that make a man a mirror

& when you gather it
(root & wort)
let no sun
shine on it

(Light steals the color of its power).

Cut it with hard, crooked iron,
turning away: unseen, unharmed.

With it you walk no evil path,
bad men turn & run, give way.

These are *eryngoes*. The power of this wort is never named as such here, but then we are never told who or what a gorgon is, in the same way we are expected to know that the North Star was sacred to Isis.

Her sistrum shook:

let joy & love attend
this toilet.
　　　　　Enter
cosmetic mistress,
merriment & music,
sovereign of
　　　　　　song & dance.

The sound of this instrument protected all those in ear range.

Up to Luper's altar
they led
           the boys

& touched their brows
with bloody blades
& wiped dark's mark away
with milk soaked
                      wool wads.

The Lupercalia survives today in the sending of Valentines. Cupid's arrow shot through a blood red heart recalls a bleeding welt.

membris valens

skinned in Pan's black
Palatine valentine den

Pan & Luper are the same. They both despise clothing & demand nakedness at all times.

Bitter mother's sea star
protects travellers:

Pass fear's night & enter this eye,
        the most & least of paradise,

        what dust brings you
        to this entry, this vortex

The sea star is the compass point, the center of things as well as their entrance. The eye opens later.
The dust is always there. The vortex reminds of 1927.

Uprooted Ganymede,
spread-eagle,
spins in terror's wing beat whirlwind.

The screaming revenger enters
hard, white,
succulent, marble nates:

god seed animates, heats
cold stone.

Son of Tros,
manhood's joy,

iron talons grip your Hellenic crotch—
the boy's loins caught,
fondled with feathery caresses.

You pour the nectar you take,
your bright cup overflows, spills,
unlocking panic's heart.

The sacred company celebrates your service.
The sight of you
swaying through their numbers
on alabaster legs,
with teasing girdle displaying
slight cheek curves
& hints of secret curls,

sets fires.

Ganymede was an attractive lad taken for a ride by an eagle. He was so much in demand & his fa-
vors so chased that the gods decided to get into the act as well. Imagine him here as a late Hellenic
statue, substantial & well turned, suspended. This action is not suitable for a stately pace because
it involves consummation & desire melting into affection.

A slim waisted Keftiu boy,
copper faced with comely thighs
in blue & gold
loin cloth
carries his *rhyton* through
Minoan halls,
full lipped & almond-eyed

His beauty, grace & shape
dazzled the archaeologist's eyes,
& hid his secret below the belt.
Today this age celebrates
this mistake
              & Psyche's night
finds us fumbling in the dark
handling light.

Keftiu were "island people from across the green seas." They steered by the stars & visited the Aegyptians often. The *Larousse Gastronomique* describes a *rhyton* as an ancient drinking vessel shaped like a ram's horn, decorated sometimes with a goat's head, lacking a flat base so that a drinker was obliged to empty its contents before setting it down. Psyche had a memorable but short lived affair with Cupid. This mistake happened in 1900 when many feel the age's beginning happened as well.

Mistletoe grows
watered with earth's tears.

Evil dreams disturb the Aesir's sleep,
bloody-eyed spooks walk round Balder's bed,

in distant Eastern forests
an aged giantess bears
a wolf brood,

a red sun stains the sky
& stars
like weary swallows at sea too long
drop & sink into the void.

Winter rushes with wind & wolves
through Valhalla's unpaid-for halls,
walls crack like broken oaths.

As the world spoils it loses its shape.

Mistletoe was once the youngest of all things in creation, therefore not responsible for its actions.
It was a common expression at the time to ask: "How's by Elves? How's by Aesir?" Balder was very
beautiful. The Eastern forests were even darker when the light failed & died. Valhalla was never
properly paid for, this created a great deal of ur-ill-feeling among the eldrich.

Heliopolian priests have brought
an eagle with painted wings
                                    & made
a spiced, palm branch nest
to burn him in alive.
                            This fiery death
as insatiable as an infant eagle's maw
leaves ashes
                    as white as bone in the nest,
snow on the cliff-ledge.

The Aegyptians had a festival for everything. When the sun moved into the center of Renaissance imagination these holidays came to light.

On the morning appointed
in dead winter,
sheep huddled in the road
between hedges,

all who live
by the Dee's edge
put out their light & heat,
grew cold,

drew love's circle
near me, enchanted,
to undo the charm,

took turns, spun the wheel.
Bobbin's friction sparked
fallow straw with fornlorn fire

to light a fir torch
that kindled peat
where each man gathered
his hearth's new flame.

The Dee is a river down the road from where I live. Its name means "holy river" & hints that there is a goddess in its waters. It joins the Rawthey which joins the Lune not far from here. In Aberdeen boys run about collecting "Peat to burn the witches, please?" It is wise to get one's cattle in when the light fails—out from under it.

Red ochre for life & strength
sprinkled over bones
buried with
        chipped flint instruments,
        shells, & a chieftain's staff
        of reindeer horn carved with
        a stag on the run,

under each head a rock.

The dead have a cult of their own with numerous followers. This list does not mention the soul's double, a stone doll, buried with the dead it insures that they will not come back. Protection must not be confused with celebration.

Dazed eyes,

  glazed by daydream webbing
as if this bonny lass'
sheer boyish beauty
were spun by Burne-Jones,
a silvery innocent,
Circe,
warms her hands at the blaze
kindled to consume her.

1722. (Near Dornoch.) She was the last witch burned in Scotland.

For moony silver, take one penny weight of
white powder, fifty pennies weight of azloth
mixed with bronze & nitre; heat & stir with
an iron rod.

Again, for sunny gold, do the same thing using
red powder.

    & the Royal Society insisted:
        James Price prove your proven leechdom,
        ripen matter before our eyes,
        work a perfection & concoct
        an observable eternity.

        & Dr Price agreed, gathered the members,
        swallowed prussic (blue) acid, collapsed
            before their eyes, died

        ars totum requirit hominem

1782. *Art requires the total man*. This can rightly be misread as *Art asks a lot of people*.

The air hums
vedas, eddas, sagas,
the lore receives
this man, the soul's periplus,
spiral entry,

Olson rests in the map of his true sight,
at the end of the world
where continents shift like vowels,
land gathers him up,
consonant energy.

1970. Words that remember a poet who died as the decade began.

ᚱᚠᚢᚠ · ᚱᛣᚲ · ᚱᛣᚲᚱ

glossed as follows:

ragna røk, røkr

Gods' doom, dusk

These or any other runes are never to be trusted. *Ragna* means powers or energies. *Røk* means fate, appointed or determined. *Røkr* was confused with *røk*, it means twilight or failing light, because its image was more memorable than *røk* the skalds slipped it in.

Neit:

I've been, am, will be
yet no man's drawn my net apart.
My shuttle wove the world,
I bore the sun before the born.

Neit's pride was swallowed by Isis in the *Golden Ass*. She was a Libyan & often kept company with gorgons.

clear stone,
crystalline eye,
Gorgon gift.

See following.

A pinch of dust outweighed the stone,
Alexander's rock,

        black eye, yellow,
        blind as terrible bats,
        mute as mice as big as foxes—

dark night.

        "Tell me wise Diogenes, what now?"

        "You stand in my light."

Alexander was a famous man once, but tends to be lost in the shuffle now. People still remember Diogenes.

Near the world's end, where waters well
       Dhul-Karnain's cook
       washed a dried fish
       in a certain spring, now lost

& in his hands
       hard black scales
       silvered, shimmered, wriggled away,

resilient white meat, once yellow sun baked,
stiff bones sprung back
       slipped through his fingers,

light caught its escape,
                danced in ripples—

    moving image of eternity.

The world's end is a place as well as an event that has occurred an innumerable number of times.

The fish of wisdom's spawning ground
        found
                in the middle & early sixties
                by Danes.
Fish diseased,
                scales, leprous white,
        blotched by rotten snows—

        Miriam's anger
flows on Avalon's waters.

These are salmon who ate hazel nuts. Miriam became very angry with her brother when she found out he had married a Negro.

Old double-horns couldn't kill his green cook
when he didn't find the trusty fish's wonder water
again (now lost)

Antiochus Epiphanes threw him overboard,
the green siren still sings,
pisces resurrected—

the most & least of paradise.

The cook swallowed where it slipped through his fingers.

What wort be brought,
which stone be struck

How goes a cure to cleanse this fish & set aright

these affairs.

This problem tends to be seasonal whether it is the fall of 1963 or the aeon of Aquarius.

Eternity's image moves, shifts
before our eyes—
                    when we were blind
    amazed, alarmed,
                        ensnared by dark corridors,

couriers brought torches.

This is the problem of focus & the trouble with orders. Although it is only a matter of sliding that makes the equinox occur a little off each year, it still confuses. Where do we lay our hands or set up crosses? Before they brought a ball of string which lead to the light, not the light itself.

The worm dreams of wings
on greeny leaf.

& the young ancient meets
the old hot foot abed

as if, scalded, he were
the patriarch Oedipus
near dead from the riddle unravelled

but for his bright eyes,
abode of the sun's chariot.

There the scintilla,
the spark of dark sight & spiral entry.

Mr Palmer & Mr Blake meet. These are said to have beeen real historical personages despite their presences. Blake is famous for his angels. Palmer is remembered for the visions that deserted him leaving in their wake a competent but less interesting sight. They returned late in Palmer's life. He serves as an inspiration to the young & inspired, as well as a warning.

Come Corybantes, sing
Aegyptian Albas
for the New
                Kingdom of Jerusalem.

The Corybantes are always on hand with their noisy, extravagant dances. Albas are sacred to Taum who is the sunset or the sun before it rises. The New Kingdom in spite of everything else always turns out to be worth it.

My starry belly bends above you
a thick white milky way explodes, flows
down your green knees, gathering
in your mossy navel, but
Shu my father separates our souls,
uncouples us at dawn.
                              Ra-Harakhte
rides across his land.

Jackals, falcons bear his scarab.
Dog-apes greet the sun.

Our hearts, torn apart, carry
the glimmering dream-wrought stone halved.

Only night can join this sun-split rock.

Sex for the Aegyptians was a ritual & desire was a preparation for death's Judgement Hall. They
went about their business creating the image all Christians call heaven. When they had finished
they left it. It must never be forgotten how important masturbation was to them; dying is a solitary
occupation in the final analysis.

THREE WHITE SCARVES
for the Kundun's fourteenth body

Into the IV seasons' stations
            feeling failing & unfailing
            smelling the growth & the rot,
Potnia, Mater moving.

Those the Lords love . . .
                              (blessed)
φῶs
& when brought to this yield
φόρος   that fate.

O to sit
            below heavy boughs & light-tremble,
eye measures mind
in an arbor, earth, root, in bud-fold
            returned, in appointed rounds

            Anna Perenna, her
            quinces & quadrupeds
            leap

Or the canals' clear air, no summer-stink
that water-way to remember, have ease in
            shadows' reflection, filagree

Or the Kundun's flight or *Those Withholding*
Youngblood, Bell,
                        travellers' & route reports
"former body so fond of horses"

As for Mao Tse-tung
(like asking a Jew in '42
                        what he thought to der Führer)
His Highness replied
                        He too shall achieve buddha-hood

I   Carved gables of a Chinese peasant's hut
     not far from a monastery's gold roof
     float in the Cho Khor Gye,
     part of the future.

     Search groups set out in the year 1937.

     The big eared boy,
     traces of second arms on his trunk,
     fondles the former body's rosary.

     They returned in the late summer, 1939.

II

Eastern, Northern
threats . . .

Lhasa's houses shake,
forty dead, dull detonations,
Earth-devils quake.

A great glow
hangs in cloudless eastern skies.

A kneaded tsampa ball rolls
from gods' dancer's golden bowl.
Yes, the slip inside.

Forty nobles, two hundred guards,
machine guns & howitzers
escort his Presence,
a dust cloud on Karo pass—

their empty rooms
unswept,

their refilled cups
undrunk.

III

Famine, the land can't feed
them all, invaders & citizens.

The Panchen Lama enters
the Holy City.

Cranes & wild geese cry,
beat wings over a cold moon.

ISIS' MEMORY

traces of the Great Herbal of Horus

"I had sight offered me in crystallo & I saw."
John Dee, 25 May 1581

Tender nibs of
    soft beans &
  peas in
their cod

   leaf & root found,

the tits of
   Isis,
     hid, dark in

catkins, acorns, walnut, almond

     quincunx secret.

       ■

  Her burdens trace the veils,
   pelts for tygers' eyes

Here the weight of his arm is a dark stranger.
Here his shin is a quarrel, a cold hearth &
his hand bending her back is an angel in disguise.

       ■

> To center the universe
> in a single night's brief dream

■

It is one thing to keep track, record the days & nights, taking comfort from such an aimless task. But still another to draw from that record a thread made up of what is lost to habit, a thread not spun from the series of events & dreams set down alone, something that is forgotten each night before sleep & each morning before rising. What seemed aimless before, sketchy & of no use becomes the pledge. To go forth & achieve the next station, a certain devotion must be held & holding it a responsibility is assumed, more clearly: consumed. This thread nets the heart.

At first the diary of day &/or dream does no more than record, but in its persistence & dullness it instills the keeper with a certain & previously unknown link to matter or *hyle*. These elements, fundamental matters, are oddly enough not part of personal perception; they come upon us unawares. They are sought indirectly by the heart.

■

> Ears, thoughts, words & the day echoes

■

& the air's hum
                        vibrant
            shines
                    aglow,

helios, the beck dries up
            & the river stones
bone dry heaps

                        rippling
of the atmosphere, gull wings
above low water—
                        shallow obscure surface
yet the gull's eye spots the fish.

                I observe this
not closely, casually, not for augury, a half-sight
                    until now as
a god shapes up in this hindsight, wings form
                the rime.

The image hums:
                Lovely god, beloved bird
                holy flight, here above
stillness in the heat
                stir the fish from dark in—
                to structure's light &
                        skim the surface of vision.
The thyme brought out from the kitchen into the sun dries,
& day's heat tints the sky rose

                    waiting for rain

Dressed in wizard robes
       Thunder's lord goes to town,
       Thunder's lord kicks up the dust.
Called by it he calls it,
       his cells flash anticipation,
a certain sense he alone has stirs
       inside his heart.
The invisible light, on clouds' edge
       shakes his arms & legs.
"He has learned to read his own symptoms"
       to be their Word
in this manifest
in his acute magic
       internal rime, vision in vision
Aware, he rises before the rest
        (nostrils & throat alive)
what isn't there yet filling the mind.
       In the lunge of the gull
right before the rain
a god-light shimmers, a shape.

       ■

       Spirit, thought
       full, right
      come thru the eyes
       free & nimble

       ■

       Tis hot & dry
     It forces the Courses & Urine
    Tis Cephalick, Uterine & Stomatick.
Tis good for Spitting of Blood & Convulsions & for Gripes.

      It cures & disposes to Sleep

       ■

Turn of furrow, tufts & plough,
Iron dips into earth
grass, clod under clod,
            line traced by the furrow
Green in the dark stretches of rock wall
            set out by boundaries
Land netted with stones

■

                  I stayed home
& read the dates & details of an old man's life
moved from room to room with book & cigarettes. How
the chronology absorbed me, event, movement, how
it ran along my own day, as much a part as
this glass of ice & bitter brown Carpano, a bright
thin bit of lemon

■

            anima, intellect
                  complete & ordered,
            move in on the eyes
            open & quick

■

& it was the occasional week-ender with ice cream
or a quick rattle of gravel outside the window—
not much more than flies or sunlight on the hedge
broke the sway my heart held to.
Such a tender, simple notion took me in arms,
            set me down

■

So a world of dream takes shape
            from the mind of images
& the soul of all things takes thought
        out of the centers they sleep within,
Anima — perpetual,
                still, asleep
So these things' souls take up my heart
            & tremble now
                    like a lapwing,
                royal, crowned
As Isis hid her child aided by the bird
                                    Pliny mentions
& the sun's soul stirring again in all things

                        ■

The branches come out of the ground in great numbers, growing
to the height of sixe foote, garnished with brave flowers of
great beautie, consisting of fower leaves in a piece, of an orient
purple colour. The cod is long & full of downie matter, which
flieth away with the winde when the cod is opened.

                        ■

                L'anima, l'intelleto
                    intero e sano
                per gli occhi ascende
                più libero e sciolto

                        ■

Thought stops yet the image persists
            Day twists till the day's form
            takes me
            & interrupts none of this joy
                only to increase, complete the shape.
Mind rests wherein the heart dwells

                        ■

                    Rosebay willow-herb
          nimble, free in my eye

     The air in August now, windy night
               tall stalks bent

     Where in this hollow, lidless silence
                does the howl begin, the shutter?

     St John's wort caught in my sight.

                    ■

Magic & botany,
& star-craft, sleepless ones,
The Watchers taught
                    their wives, men's daughters
to make swords, to make-up their faces.

Wisdom from above, god-seed spent
                    from above

From this the lore grows, sprouts,
                    day & her labors
We got secrets: Cattle, then field
                    sky sleeps on ground
inside her turnings
                    warm intimacies

Mystery, earth & her axis,
soil clings to its pivot, spins
above the blackthorn hedges,
                    along shadows
                         down to the river
lapwings hum, circling,
          light near a red cow.

A flap in the wild grass,
     a young rook with blue eyes.

Fledgling
& racket in the rookery branches

                    ■

My broken utterance
        my mouth, my trembling word
What speech, my anima mundi,
        how spoken as you speak it
                when I open to you in a tongue trill
swallowing you

Where my foot falls ajuga grows
                        & wild garlic
        & words swell with May's signature

                    ▪

Or did it spring forth just so,
bright as Hestia's hearth,
                    hot, true?
Home's dame, lights of the prytaneum,
        dark melts in air around you

                    ▪

Net of fragments half-begun.

Still the image delivers this chaos
even if bits & phrases imitate my loves.
No, I loose nothing to homage,
                but begin made anew

sure enough, I am new
            though my voice answers, repeats

                    ∎

Sun & wind
        the smell, estragon, of another country
& the field
                spread with shit

                    ∎

O mouse, keep this granary
now rhubarb shades rocks in the garth
summer lays down
                  on the fells

O mouse, keep this greenery
each of the rusted seeds

        This creature sacred to sunlight
        swifter than the arrows of his master

gray, long-tailed

provident & curious familiar

                   ■

       Soul, reason
           inbetween yet set,
       rise in the eyes
       spacious but perceived

                   ■

Fairies, weasels, rats & ferrets
or seven fat geese in a field
        hissing, brown & white,
their eyes follow me, turn,
        beaks ruffle grass, feathers—
the sun, the road I walk on slope.

Heifers, wary sheep my familiars;
to take vision from animal gazing
        through a door underground.
The very devil dazzles such glances,
        all motion stops in these tracks.

The Eternal City's heart
        as common as dirt.

Not man, but his image.

                   ■

As his hint & trace air out sun-lit places,
his torso of terror on terrace & lawn
spins up musics in dusty places
from whir of wings or fumbling of fawn;
& his weird wild lightning eye quivering
in clean gardens is unnerving.
The well chosen words, conversations' paces,
all heartless babble, stop & are gone.

■

In the middle of the road
I startled a red ring
of fox cubs attacking
a black cat.

They broke away,
hid in the thickets.
Should I kill the cat
out of mercy or
let the cubs return
& leave fate interrupted
but undisturbed.

■

Dull clouds fade the leaf-shadow's
                         dark stalks
their gentle droop, heavy, but canopied,
                         something of summer.
Rhubarb, the Volga's barbarous plant.
What does this early harvest bring?
fiberous terra-cotta puree,
blood cleansed by spring's tonic.

After the ten days of sorrow
     seeking the lost & dark maid,
     coming disguised in her grief
Demeter arrives at Eleusis.

A single green ear of corn
         reaped in silence.
Eleusis
Past now, Alaric sacked the halls, 395 ad
Eleusis   this lost, scattered.

To walk those 14 miles with noisy crowds
     amid the laughter in dust-cloud

At this place an advent
on the road down by the river I see by morning sun
     not water, but ripple's glitter
Above the scar in dark bracken is heather
Earth's colors shift in the eye, *epopteia*
     a drama in the aura
So yesterday morning when we walked down
a cloud of flies
     hovered above us, following
in ears, eyes, hair.

Must've been the end of a cycle . . .
the close warmth brought them
         not Lammas
          but a later harvest;
marked "Help Wanted", *Boedromion*
   —Sept, New Year

Hippolytus called it a light's spark
     a glimpse
   of an unseen
      season's link.
Strength in his naked back, dark face
lifts the hay & ahead at dusk
     on the Sedbergh road
three trucks with three tiers of sheep
     leave the dale, fields empty.
In the headlights a rabbit, an owl on a fence post.
Mystery folds the heart,
     single images add up.
Simple observation initiates us. The task at hand.

These labors our advent.
The calender in the fields fashions hidden celebrations.
First leaf flowering, ripe corn
                    thrice-ploughed
wind in leaves or light rain
                    & the haying done as of last week
Demeter manifest in this, Triptolemus
                    knew her by sight.
The dogs still bark, never know us,
                    the calves expect food
yet we come this way every morning;
                    nothing changes
                              but the rose hips are riper
& the cow parsley taller, thicker stalked,
                    the light later
on Helms Knott.
                    hiera brought forth,
a hedgehog blinded by the car lights
                    red-eyed & slow.
deiknymena, things revealed

                    ▪

    barley water with mint,
            Iambe's dirty joke

                    ▪

waybread's broad green leaves push up
even through the asphalt on the drive.
There's a lust in this greeness
                    something that overcomes,
the strong gives birth to the strong,
made a eunuch by hemlock
                              not like Attis,
the priest cries,
what is born of spirit
                    has a strength beyond flesh.

Mother of Corn, Anger, another of your names,
            your sorrow, our mercy,
bears the baby on the fan, Brimus, Iacchus—

& we, come from the sea, having bathed the pig,
            in light seeking dark

Poetry is that Art, that branch of magic & kabbalistic root that celebrates *presence* or simply *there*. Pointed to, referred to & indicated away from the speaker, other than, in that language remains the initial phenomenon of the poet. Poetry begins in *the,* that quick almost silent signal of presence.

By "begins" I mean something like the moment before the silence is broken. The Hebrews began their alphabet with a letter in which we see the mystery of the open throat & poised tongue, it had no sound & was voiceless yet represented the phenomenon of utterance. & the most astonishing fact on which poetry thrives is that every sentence (or projected unit of utterance) once begun *CAN stop*, not complete itself & begin again as a new sentence related or unrelated to its own initial impulse or sound. No where else in the cosmos is this aspect of *will* & magic so clearly & precisely manifest.

Poetry celebrates not only presence but the multiplicity of presence & the infinite possibilities of *there*. The poem has the power of location, it is a place—an actual (not metaphorical!) spacial event of language which begins in the mouth & lungs & moves outward into time, the mind, the body. There it starts, flirts, catches the imagination with abstraction & the ear with concrete patterns, shifts & comes back changing the abstract into the concrete &

■

Eleusis,
advent

■

If a man's feet swell on a journey, take this wort;
pound with vinegar, then bathe the feet with it &
smear them. Soon they will grow smaller.

THE SEVEN OF CUPS

Phantasms rise from the cups—wreaths, gems, serpents, sorrow, monsters & towers—all cloud borne. A man in black contemplates them.

"In the most holy of mysteries, before the presence of the god the impulsive forms of certain terrene daemons appear, which call the attention from undefiled advantages to matter."
Proclus

I   *The sorrowing face*

She works a song from her sorrow, her longing & painful wandering. Her husband went away, out over the tossed waves. She can not sleep, but wakes before dawn each morning, wondering where on this earth he is. So, being alone, having no friends, she seeks a lover but her husband's kin plot against her with dark thoughts. They want to separate the woman from her new love, make her live alone again, far from his side in pain. She longs for her lover now. Her husband had wanted her to live at home, but there was no one there she loved, no good friends.

One day she finds her lover unhappy, sad at heart, & hiding his feelings from her, pretending to be carefree. They had vowed only death would separate them. But this changes & now their love becomes something that never was. She must live with his hate everywhere she goes.

Her husband's kin make her live in the woods, under an oak tree in a cave. The halls of the earth are old & she is all longing.

The valleys are dim, the hills high & the bitter hedges of the city overgrown with briars. There the homes are joyless. Love's flight makes her sad. While others have beds to lie in at dawn, she goes to her hole under the oak & sits on long summer days. She weeps for her wandering & her pain. Never will her heart let her rest from the care & longing of her life.

She curses her lover with a heavy heart & carefree face to hide it, & constant sorrow. May he be his only joy in this world. May he be sent off to a far country with her husband to sit under rock cliffs chilled by storms & circled by water. There may they both remember happier homes.

It is hard to live one's life longing for love.

II   *The fallen towers*

Fate broke the well wrought stone wall, the castles decay. The giants' work crumbles. Roofs fell in, the towers ruined, their gate grates plundered. Ice is on the lime, the shelter is in shards, shattered, & collapsed. Age ate it away & earth's grasp, the ground's hard grip, holds the master builders.

More than once this wall, lichen gray & red stained, stood in storms & lasted, kingdom after kingdom. A quick thought conceived it. In ingenious rings, the brave bound the wall roots together with wonder & wire. The castle halls were bright & had many baths, high horned towers.

The great noise of troops & men's joy filled them until wild fate upset it all.

Wide walls crumble & the plague comes. Death does away with the brave swordsmen. Their ramparts become wastelands. The city crumbles & those who would rebuild it lie dead in the ground. The halls crumble & the cinnabar arch's round roof work is stripped of its tiles. The ruins fall to the ground, broken into heaps, where long ago many men with glad hearts, bright with gold, adorned & gleaming, proud & hot with wine shined in their armor. There in this broad kingdom's castle they saw treasure, silver & precious gems, wealth, possessions & costly stones.

Stone halls once gushed with hot steam. The wall held it all in its bright bosom. There were many baths & there was ease. Water poured over gray rocks in hot streams filling round pools. That then was a kingly thing.

III   *The precious stones*

The garnet's heart, whatever the hue, is always regular & its colors follow the changes of fire: blood red, orange, & green. When God's anger flooded the earth, this gem's blaze was the only light the Patriarch Noah had aboard his ark. The stone is sometimes softer, sometimes harder than crystal. It protects men from evil, casts fearful dreams from their sleep, & worn on the body, keeps the skin pure. Widows wear hairpins & necklaces of garnets. This gem brings men love, faithfulness & safety from all wounds. When danger draws near its fire grows dim.

Jet, the black & velvet stone, resembles coal. It was first found by the river Gangai in the land of Lycia. Pounded to a fine dust & burnt in fire, this gem will drive off all dragons & snakes. Its healing power soothes aches in the head & teeth, cures epilepsy, comforts pains in the belly & draws out water sickness, dropsy. It also takes away all charms & spells cast on a man or his house. The English believe that jet protects them from thunder, devils, poison, & witchcraft. Irish wives burn this black-stone in their husbands' absence to assure their safe return. Beetles worked from it cause the Evil Eye to look away from all Romans.

Time runs rings around this gem. Spiders fly from the red agate & the green cures eyes while the brown one gives the warrior victory, brings the rich man wealth, heals the infirm & secures favor for the lover in his lady's sight. It also increases a man's cunning & wit. If a woman drinks water that has washed a green agate, she will always be fruitful. The Aegyptians are fond of the gray kind & often wear it around their necks to prevent stiffness, colic, & diarrhoea. There are certain agates in which moss grows, these are placed by farmers on their right arm & on the right horn of their oxen in order to bring great harvests.

Amber, like Aphrodite, is born of the sea's foam. It is one of the most ancient of gems & was worn by the first peoples on this earth. Homer, in his books, tells us that the Phoenicians used it as money. A certain kind that is washed up on the shores of Sicily glows with a blue or green flame. Its powers are mysterious & for the most part unknown. The dust shaved off this stone, mixed with honey & rose oil soothes sore ears & restores dim sight. Taken in water, it aids the liver, kidney & removes belly aches. A small phallus worked from amber protects its maker from all devils including the Evil Eye. A little piece put on the nose checks bleeding & placed on a large swelling of the neck, will shrink it. In some countries it is used to ward off witches, warlocks, & bad luck. The Arab leeches use it often as medicine & in the Orient it is carved in the form of small lions, fish, dogs, frogs, & hares which are thought to make men more manly & women more fruitful.

Some wise men believe salt to be the most precious of stones, it is certainly the most sacred. Its power both heals & preserves all manner of things. Offered to the gods, it keeps a man in their favour & free from all evil. Salt is most used by farmers & priests as it purifies both the field & the temple, while assuring the success of all acts performed in these places. Wise Moses wrote that the number of the word *salt* in his tongue is equal to the secret name of God. Life & death end & begin with this precious substance. The Abyssinians so prize it that they use it as their money.

Crystal is a form of ice, while not as cold as common ice, it never melts. Only the purest water will freeze into this limpid stone. The power of the sun can be directed through its clarity & thereby heal the eyes & heart of men. Carved into spheres it is highly prized by all men in the East & the West. Some say that by gazing into the center of a crystal sphere one may perceive all things in time & place as they shift. Crushed & mixed with honey, this stone will increase the milk in a mother's breasts. The water that has washed a crystal can be given to cattle & men to drink & will cure them of disease. The souls of the dead & quick, it is said, dwell in this ancient ice.

The Aegyptian Thoth & Greek Hermes protect the powers of chalk. The deliberate mark of this stone is more useful than its simple presence. If a man writes the initials of the three kings, Caspar, Melchior, & Balthazar, on his door, his house will be safe from witches & fire. Of all the gems this is the most secret, only through use can a man come to understand it.

IV   *The laurel wreath*

Leaves of the sweet bay tree bring consolation as well as peace. Their green, almost black, surfaces seal up a powerful & godly sap which produces visions & oracular frenzies. The leaves of this wreath are picked on Mount Parnassus where the sweet bay flourishes & is sacred to Apollo.

To wear this crown is to be honored, assigned to triumph & renown. But to seek this green tribute is to sip death's waters.

V   *The writhing basilisk*

The dragon or basilisk has the power to hear through its eyes. A man seen or heard by this creature instantly becomes its victim, but if he were to escape, it is said, that he would have looked upon a thing with a camel's head, a deer's horns, rabbit's eyes, cow ears, the neck of a snake, a frog's belly, carp scales, hawk claws, & a tiger's pads. The dragon lives in the depths of water & the blackness there.

All of the earth we live on is marked with this beast's form. Its trunk & limbs can be seen in mountains & hills, its veins & arteries run through rock. Dragon's breath hovers in every place, it is important to locate it at all times. Its hidden presence must always be sought by man, for it affects him just as the contour of the land does.
The creature guards a great treasure. In its forehead, above the space between the eyes, just beneath the scales, there lies a hard congealed mass that is called dragon's stone. It is the beast's second brain, its link to air, & must be removed while the dragon still breathes. This dull gem heals all sickness & bestows immortality on its owner. The fat from its heart brings luck in law suits, & its teeth placed in a goatskin bag make a gift fit for kings.

VI   *The coiled snake*

The coils of this snake have no beginning, no end; just as the seasons pass, the skin covering them will be shed. This long legless creature is in all places, visible & invisible. Its eyes are lidless & have the power to bring sleep.

The snake is the guardian of all things underground, roots, jewels, & springs. It is the master of silence & motion.

VII   *The veiled figure*

Three women reach their destination, a bright palace built of high steel walls, circled by iron gates, each held fast by heavy bars. The giants' labor was never so great as when this building rose, never had their breasts heaved such sighs, never since then had rivers of fire flowed so freely from their burning furnaces. Ivory covers every entry, each roof, fastened with brass, is held aloft by amber columns.

Here in these lovely halls she sits, comforting the tedious day with her song as she works the quick loom, waiting for their return. Her needle draws the elements' birth & order, displays the laws nature used to tame the first confusion, when her mother's hand set each unset principle. The subtle matters rise, the heavy sink, diaphanous aether floats, ocean swells, & earth's image hangs in the heavens.

She weaves the web with many colors: stars glitter in gold, the waters flow as indigo & bright gems stud the rocky shores. As the eyes imagine the tossing waves, the ears seem to catch the water's murmer as it breaks upon sands & dashes seaweed against rock cliffs. Her threads & craft are that cunning.

She forms five zones. The first, the red woof, shows parched, dry land burned by fierce suns. Softer shades glow through the second two, here it is temperate & man may live. The last, woven from dark, somber colors, lay over both poles & hides them in constant cold.

She lifts the veil to display her handicraft as a man in black enters the room. The maid is a bride & the three women hurry through the halls to wait on her marriage.

KNUCKLEBONES

Anna versus
                           for Robert & Helen

. . . wild high rose,
         sweet gum ooze

           caught by
bright net,
               luna's tray

& steps
       swept clean

& bread crumbs in corners.

A simple meal, wood plates,
a rough beaujolais
                     & silver goblet.

May you be safe
              in the light of your house.

As we're each called to attend the eclipse

This morning the post brought
a wing ripped from a strychnine poisoned chicken.

A few feathers fall on the mat
caught up in a cold, late wind.
I am accused.

Tonight Barbara Buvée
stalks my dreams in black 17th century robes,
carries a stolen host & crystal dildo to
Juno's chambers through hypnotic halls.

The chalk white women giggle
& smear their bald heads, forelocks & faces
with milk.

I blow a mouth of water over the wing,
this cools the craft afoot, but the knot tied
asleep, awake can't be cut—
the call's gone out.

I answer yet weep for the changes:

the single fish vanishes in the rapid beck,
the red tulips no longer dance in the cool kitchen,
they fade like hearts on green stalks,
their wrinkled petals yawn replies.

Some other music melts the frost & pokes the fire.
Some one else closes the door &
prepares the afternoon this morning.

Lusty sparrows,
                    eddies of still air
toss up dust & leaves, straw.

These are ancient fragments,
older than the first frost.

. . . these are islands,

asters, gentians, bright
sumac, wild grape

                    clusters
or inner regions of defence,
escape.

Across the road light ripens
an ochre field, down the hill
bees cling to the purple asters'
last stalks.

The ground thick with
crickets, thickets & thorn.
Coming up the rise, I turned,
at the top vines fell heavy with

deep, sweet grapes,
hard seeds & gray dust.

Summer fails,
darkling shadows sharpen the atmosphere.

The bees have fled from under the sumac.

Kiva in clear light.
Gran Quivira just a ruin in the sun,
 see here, rock-face deity.
No mano grinds metate, gold maize,
 noon, as we walk, settles on the cholla;
 heat-ripples rise, above hills, feet kept to the path.
Sift, sift, shuffle, step, on red adobe
            by one-seed juniper,
"cedar", wind-rustle, with frequent stops;
 rubble of ivory rocks, gray-green in shadows.
A purple blossom on the cane stuck in sand;
& on the deep, darkened floor of the hole,
            dust covered & pillared, a snake curled
rattling in a still rhythm:
                    hiss . . . chu!
& they climbed down the ladder & saw it there;
            as the yucca, the yucca, shook:
Hush!
            An old god wakes up.
            An old god wakes us.
            Sky & land are here.
& they climbed down the ladder,
            the late afternoon sun
casting shadows in the hole;
dark feet stepped off rungs onto dark ground;
caught in hesitation,
            as fire burned the saltbush
to make their meal blue.
            . . . a snake shook:
Yes, hush, god-hiss!

Rock & root cunning

for Basil Bunting

This wort has seed
like an adder's head,

long stiff leaves,
thin & thorny,
that send out stalks,

between the leaves
are brown blossoms,
between the blossoms

are seed as we said before
like an adder's head:

its root is
small & dark.

This stone has been inlaid
with the body's sea (salt
blood) & a runner made
from wood with it, bored
by gimlet.

Who of the rune-hoard
comes to man's land?

The trusty fish that swims the body's stream;
the bird, screaming if he tears a corpse, is born

a revenger. The stone
not reached by sun,
not cut with knife.

The body's rune, stiff seas & adder's hoard;
this rock & root unreached by some.

At Alexandria saints
drowned in the sea,

took flight to heaven in flames

& Saint Anthony
(who'd had enough
of Lombardy)

withdrew,

later to go in a calm
repose to God.

His body gloried day by day
in miracles
(in particular

deliverance
of the possessed.)

Naked & greased up,
olive oiled, old licorous
Sophocles danced
with his cloak on.

The way his leg bent
made them horny:
what Plato meant by,

Poetry is no good kid,

& the patron meant by,

Hands off,
leave my boys alone.

Ten love notes

Even Eros
stops,

caught
midair

by your
eyes.

I
my skin burns
my eyes cloud
my ears ache

I sweat
I shake

II
the stone softens,
starts to vanish

III
you are sweeter
than unwatered wine

IV
just one glance
burns my heart out

V
your body,
soft as marrow

VI
soft, ripe thighs
untouched flesh

VII
you are mine,
the down on your leg as well

VIII
dice cast,
heart lost

IX
our winks
waste a good thing

X
soon,
you'll pour
your own drink

ΠΟΙΚΙΛΟΣ

for Guy Davenport, μυθόπλοκον

                              hyacinth-
hue

                       song-filled head
washed ashore

                                    sea-
dyed

                 sprawled on dry land
                   tangled in sea weed
        dumb as an unbroken wave

                              rock
& hoary sea's
off spring

                              salt

water wound four times

& chick peas grew gold
                          on shore
    you come from the edge of earth
                    with a gold wound
ivory handled

                              sword

clack of
         figwood testicles
sways of
                  deer skin
         phallos

             leave the mud
                          unstirred

        beside cool water
        wind murmers in the apple sprays
        leaves shiver, heavy sleep slips

        down

                    embroidery
                       earth
                 flower-crowned

                          with air's son

                                    dew

        deer grass grows

for the gods have buried

life's secret

    hidden it underground from men

white beans

    green roasted groats

        honey comb

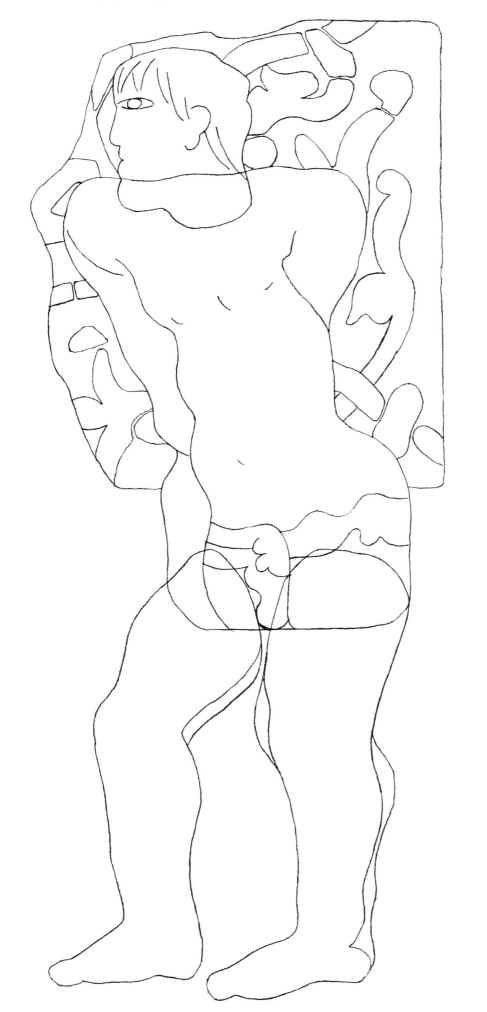

dear mother I fumble the threads

                Aphrodite &
a slim lad
                                            have
tangled me
                        with love

at the mill they grind

        honey yellow grain

                        sun

light, ripe cucumbers

        apples & pears

skin
clad

      I know all birds' tunes

bring the clear twang again

talk turtle-box

                pain-bringer
                yarn-spinner

bring my song's tale

pour the delicate gold cups

    joy & nectar joined

                  bites of
cucumber

              summer's
plump bloom

          ripe
soft enough

lettuces & pot-baked bread
            heaped up

skin
honey yellow

        dressed in
        fair
        sheer cloth

across the foot a leather strap
      covered in fair Persian

embroidery
        colors all twisted

a fire
that burns away sight

                such
                  eyes

           suddenly

with bitter, pitiless black
pitch & cedar smoke

                 light
arrows
bright

               glamor

held by a gold chain
    of tender chalk flowers
        to hold you
            my love

no bee
        nor honey for me

my tears
drop

they no longer walk on sweet
feet

all night caught my eyes

to sleep on a
friend's

                soft breasts

moon gone
               pleiades set
the hours come & go

          I sleep alone

The Jargon Society
wishes to thank the following
who are among patrons to this edition:

Mr. and Mrs. Donald B. Anderson, *Roswell*
Shelley M. Brown, M.D., *New York City*
Mr. and Mrs. W.H. Ferry, *Scarsdale*
David Fromkin, *New York City*
Thomas A. Gray, *Winston-Salem*
Drewry Hanes, *Modena*
William Masselos, *New York City*
William Barnabus McHenry, *New York City*
John Russell, *New York City*
John Sandoe, *London*

Of this edition of 1000 copies on Mohawk Superfine paper, pressman EA, using Olympus types set by EB, MB, GD, EH & GW, and designed by A D Moore of Champaign, there are 900 copies bound in paper, not numbered; 50 copies hand bound with paper over boards and numbered 1 through 50; and 50 copies hand bound in cloth over boards using handwoven cloth prepared expressly for this edition and numbered I through L. This is copy number

THE UMBRELLA OF AESCULAPIUS contains an introduction by Robert Kelly; hence, we spare you the usual commercial exhortation on the back of the book. . . However, a modest reminder that two of Thomas Meyer's books are still available. THE BANG BOOK is an erotic cowboy-ghost-story in the form of a poem. "A work of boy genius like the early symphonies of Mendelssohn"— Robert Duncan. Drawings by John Furnival. Available from *The Jargon Society*, Elm Street, Millerton, New York 12546. Cloth: $6.50; paper: $3.95. . . POIKILOS (a section of the present volume, granted, but a superbly produced piece of work) is available from *The Stonewall Press*, Box 889, Iowa City, Iowa 52240. Cloth only: $5.00. . . Thomas Meyer's next books include ANN LEE LEADS THE WAY; URANIAN ROSES; THE HERBARIUM OF THE PSEUDO-APULEIUS; THE BOOK OF JONATHAN; and OVERSEAS & HOMECOMING.

The Canadian artist, Paul Sinodhinos, now resident in London, has made the fourteen line drawings for THE UMBRELLA OF AECULAPIUS. Cricket and horse racing are two subjects often explored in his paintings. He also does portraits and conversation pieces.

A current catalogue of publications is available from *The Jargon Society*, Elm Street, Millerton, New York 12546. Photography and poetry are the concerns. Some of the names are Ralph Eugene Meatyard, Lyle Bonge, Doris Ulmann, Lorine Niedecker, Paul Metcalf, James Broughton, Basil Bunting, Alfred Starr Hamilton, Ross Feld, Thomas A. Clark, Douglas Woolf, Ronald Johnson, and Simon Cutts.

Jonathan Williams,
Director

Paperback Edition of 900: $7.50
Cloth Edition: 50 @ $27.50
Paper over boards: 50 @ $17.50